Mealtime

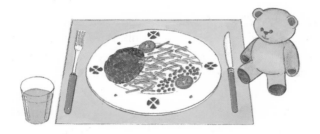

A ZEBRA BOOK

Written by Wendy Boase
Illustrated by David Bennett

PUBLISHED BY
WALKER BOOKS
LONDON

Playing makes you hungry.

running and jumping

skipping

What else makes you hungry?

It's time to eat.

washing
your hands

collecting
the table mats

What do you do at mealtime?

sitting at the table

How many people are sitting at this table?

Lots of things are on the table.

knife   fork   spoon

plate   glass

cup   salt   pepper

How do you use all these?

Your tummy rumbles when you are hungry.

a little meal for a little tummy rumble

a medium-sized meal for a
medium-sized tummy rumble

an enormous meal for an
enormous tummy rumble

Can you name these foods?

Now you eat. Tuck in!

soup

vegetables

How do you eat spaghetti?

Not with your hands!

You use your hands to eat some foods.

cheese

bread

biscuit

apple

What else can you eat with your hands?

Imagine a seven-decker sandwich.

How would you eat this?

Sharing a feast with your friends.

Have you ever had a feast?

Here are some special treats.

strawberries

ice cream

lollipop

Easter egg

What colour are they?

When do you eat special cakes?

There are lots of other things to eat.

soft banana

crunchy carrot

delicious
chocolate
pudding

sour lemon

Which of these do you like?

Who else gets hungry?

ducks

dog

cat

who else?

You drink when you are thirsty.

milk

cocoa

orange juice

water

What is your favourite drink?

drinking from a bottle

drinking through a straw

Mealtime is over.

Who helps clear up?

Where do all the pots and pans go?

What happens next?

sweeping
up crumbs

brushing
your teeth

How does your tummy feel now?